The three lives of King Bharata...

Tulika Singh

Illustrated by

Manish Das

Shiv Prakash

Della Book World
New Delhi - 110002

Disclaimer

While the author doesn't make any claims for the fool proof authenticity of all facts and timelines, intention of the book is to introduce King Bharat and Jadbharat muni to the readers in a fun and light manner.

Find more of similar books on www.ashwathatreebooks.com

First Published in 2022
ISBN : 978-93-85719-37-0

Published by **Abhishek Goel** on behalf of

Delta Book World
G-4, Prahlad House
4832/24, Ansari Road
New Delhi - 110 002 (India)

Ph. : 011-2328 8140, 4707 2321
E-mail : deltabookworld@gmail.com

PRINTED IN INDIA

Bharata brought the young deer to his hermitage and started taking care of it diligently. Seeing its mother pass away in front of his eyes, Bharata took care of the baby with a lot of compassion and love in his heart. He took charge of all its well being from feeding, to cleaning, bathing and playing with him.

Bharata would take it to green pastures and narrate divine stories while lying there. He would sing bhajans (devotional songs) to him and perform yajnas while the deer sat near him all the while. Fearful that the baby might be attacked by other wild animals he always kept the baby deer close to him. Sometimes even at the expense of ignoring his daily rituals and chores.

With passage of time, Bharata's attachment to the deer had grown multifold. Now he was more anxious of its well-being and fearful of losing it. He would often be grief-stricken by slightest pain or injury to the deer.

One rainy afternoon, Bharata was taking his afternoon nap and the deer lazed around him on the ground. Dark grey clouds covered the forest sky, the earth emanated its aromatic earthy smell. Bharata had dozed off after a long day of rituals and play. There came a group of other deers near the hermitage and the baby deer got up to watch them and soon he joined them in grazing green grass and playing with them. Soon they were faraway in the valley and the hermitage was left behind.

When Bharata woke up, his eyes searched for deer but finding his hermitage unusually quiet, he got up with a foreboding fear. With his heart beating fast, Bharata searched the places near his hermitage, at the brook, in the nearby valley but with no obvious signs of deer. His heart felt a gripping fear of loss and tears rolled down his face. He looked around the forest, but the sun was already going to set, painting adieu to the green valley.

Bharata sat with his face down, feeling his life to be worthless without the deer. His mind slipped from the path of the divine, he lost all his senses and fell to the ground. His body couldn't tolerate the pain of longing and separation. Death approached him and Bharata passed away with the name of baby deer as his last words.

The Holy Bhagavad Gita says whatever our last thoughts are at the time of our death, our next life is decided by that and hence Bharata the great emperor, who had renounced his kingdom, his sons and wealth in search of the divine was born as a deer in his next life.

In his new birth, Bharata still remembered his previous life - how he had renounced all his kingdom and pleasures and dedicated his life to the thoughts of the lord, how his days and nights were preoccupied with divine thoughts until the deer came and he got so attached to it that he has been born as an animal in this life.

Thus remembering all his doings of his previous life, Bharata-deer left his mother deer and his place of birth and moved to the ashram of Rishi Pulastya and Pulaha.

He stayed there aloof from the company of others, feeding on dry grass and roots etc, trying to exhaust the fruits of his doing. At last when his last days came he abandoned his deer body in the holy river near the ashrama.

Sometime later Bharata was again born in a family of a learned Brahman. He was the youngest of nine other brothers who were noted for their conduct, knowledge in Vedas and good looks. All being so steeped in knowledge, the pressure to learn and perform was hard on Bharata, but he who was already in divine bliss remained indifferent to all efforts.

Being the youngest, he was his parents favourite and they did all attempts to coax Bharata to learn, chant, and take up responsibilities but Bharata kept a dis-interested demeanour, as if he was dumb to all the learnings. He rarely spoke or associated with anyone, not even children of his age. For long hours he would sit in one corner and keep staring at one point. His older brothers seeing him sit like a dumb boy all day long started calling him Jadbharata.

(Jad means root, just like a tree that doesn't move from a place)

With passage of time, Jadbharata's parents passed away and his elder brothers and his wife couldn't tolerate his madness and his stone like presence in their life and they soon threw him out of the house.

Jadbharata was happy to be with himself. In his heart he always wanted to be away from emotional attachments and bondages they created. He flew like a free bird eating, sleeping wherever he wanted. Always lost in thoughts of the divine, he was mostly to be found in deep forests or dark caves in the jungles.

One day it was very late at night, Jadbharata was resting under a tree. A group of bandits who were trying to appease Bhadrakali, were looking for a human sacrifice. Right then, they sighted a well built, tall Jadbharata who was all alone sitting under a tree. They quickly encircled him and tied him with a rope, pulling him with force. They realized that Jadbharata was not at all resisting, he was neither fearful nor cried for help. He easily followed the bandits to the temple.

Reaching the temple with this strange man, the bandits bathed him, put garlands on him and anointed his body with vermillion, thus preparing him for the sacrifice. All through the rituals,

Jadbharat remained unmoved and emotionless giving jitters to the bandits.

The robber chieftain fed a tasty meal to Jadbharata. Then they put a garland and sat in front of Bhadrakali placing his head on a wooden platform. One of the bandits picked up the shining sword to perform the ritual of offering his head.

As soon as the bandit raised his hand, Bhadrakali appeared with a deafening cry. She snatched the sword from the robber's hands, cut his head and roared out loud. Seeing this, the bandit's other companions fled. Jadbharata, unaffected by the appearance of the goddess, walked away indifferently.

Once King Rahugan was on his way to Sage Kapila's hermitage, he was looking for an enlightened master who could show him the path to the truth.

One of the four bearers carrying the palanquin fell sick on the way. So, the king ordered his men, "Bring someone who is energetic to carry the palanquin." The servants saw Jadbharata on the way. He appeared to be physically sturdy and ideal for the job, so he joined the king's palanquin bearers and started walking very carefully with them.

Jadbharata walked in awareness, sometimes slow and sometimes brisk, preventing stepping on any worms or ants.

The Palanquin was going out of balance and was making the king rock from one side to another. Angrily the king blurted 'O, lazy ones, why can't you walk straight?'. The Kahars replied,

'Maharaj, we are walking with caution, but this new Kahar creates a disturbance in our movement'. His feet rises and staggers.

King Rahugan cautioned Jadbharat and said, "Brother, why don't you walk properly? Follow my command carefully, otherwise I will punish you severly."

Hearing Rahugan's statement, Jadbharat looked at him intently. He smiled and said, 'You can punish the body for sure, but I am not a body but a soul. The soul is beyond both punishment and rewards.'

Hearing such divine words from an ordinary human, the king got down from the palanquin and sat down on his knees 'Mahatma, forgive me. Please tell who you are. Are you Kapil Muni or some demigod?'

Jadabharata replied, 'Rajan! I am neither Kapil Muni nor any sage. I myself was a king in a previous life. My name was Bharata, very near to enlightenment, I got attached to a baby deer and so was born a deer next life.

In a company of a devotee, a baby deer can become a Rahugan King, and a slight oversight can drop you from your path of spirituality.

So you see, our soul keeps changing bodies according to our karma. The body is not the truth but the eternal soul which is there all the time is the only unchanging truth. If you really want enlightenment, learn the essence of the soul and you will never be born again.

Thus Jadbharata passed the ultimate knowledge to the king and finishing it, he walked away into oblivion with an air of indifference.

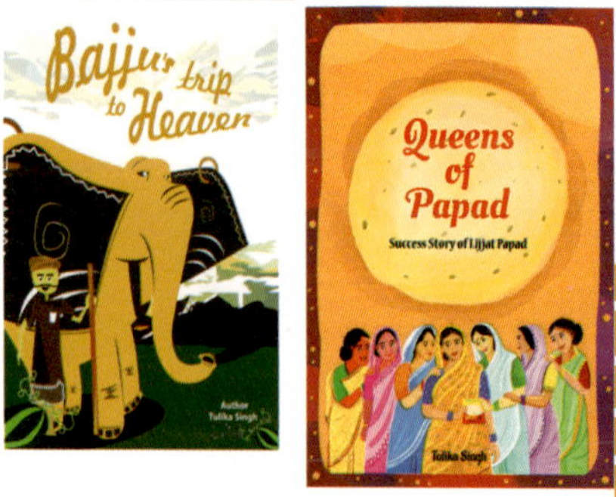

ASHWATHA TREE
Tomorrow is Us

TULIKA SINGH
Director

9625960268
mail@ashwathatreebooks.com
www.ashwathatreebooks.com
Ashwatha Tree Creations PVT. LTD.